Planet Au

A RELATABLE JOURNEY INTO NAVIGATING AUTISM

Jasmine Shepherd

Print ISBN: 979-8-35094-185-2
Ebook ISBN: 979-8-35094-186-9

Library of Congress Control Number:

Any references to historical events, real people, or real places are used fictitiously. Names, characters, and places are products of the author's imagination.

Front cover image by Ricky A. Wall

Printed by BookBaby.com, in the United States of America.

First printing edition 2023.

Jasmine Shepherd

jasmine041191@gmail.com

DEDICATION

To my super amazing, no BS taking, Lego loving, daily hugging, positive energy ray of light, my beautiful soul of a son; Jamari, my Mars.

Thank you for radiating true love, patience and resilience.

I love you until infinity and beyond

To my beautiful, diva mother, Mars 'Gigi'

Thank you for your unconditional love and guidance

Love you, Queen Mother

Contents

1

WELCOME TO PLANET AUTISM

I would like to believe that every parent of Autism has a "Moment of realization". It's not a doctor's diagnosis, it's not your mother pointing out to you something she noticed while with your child…it's a moment of realization for yourself. You realize Something is different, something is happening. I can not quite put my finger on it, but something is going on.

For myself, it was the day I realized my son was not interested in coloring books. I went out to the store one day and like any mom or parent, saw something for my child that he did not necessarily need but felt it would be a great first experience, a coloring book.

I have never gotten my son a coloring book before, and I remember the design was 'Spider-Man', so I knew he was going to absolutely love this. I grab the coloring book along with a new set of crayons. When I returned home, I set the coloring book and crayons on the area rug as I was preparing for us both to sit down and color together.

I briefly left the room to use the restroom and upon return I am dumbfounded to see a pile of consistent, finely torn pieces of paper all in a thick mountain of its own with only the laminated cover untouched. It looked as if he ran it through a paper shredder.

Imagine my disbelief. Imagine my initial confusion. He was very calm, sitting next to his creation. A thousand questions ran through my mind.

How can a tiny one and a half-year-old tear this book with such precision? I realized after some time, that it was not just the pieces that he was creating with his hands, but also, it was the soothing sound of 'the tear' that made him go so hard (stemming). I remember shedding a tear because my heart felt something.

Dots were connecting, ideas were aligning. I told myself, 'I have to find out what's going on'.

My son is different, and he is magical. From that moment on, I have not seen our life being anything but a beautiful bliss of challenges and triumphs.

Diving into the library and researching my son's habits was first on my list. I visited two libraries, one bigger than the other, scouring for information on behaviors, patterns, child development, but, nothing stood out for autism. My next turn was the internet, which yielded more results than I could process. The hours turned into days of searching and filtering through articles and YouTube videos and I eventually landed on a 'at-home' assessment for an autism screening. That initial screening opened the door for us to begin our autism journey.

I hope to inspire, encourage and be as relatable as possible to any parent, family member or caregiver who is beginning their autism journey. It can be challenging in the beginning, but you are not alone. Most importantly, there is help and your rockstar will be able to grow and develop. My most important factor is that WE can be all we can be for our children, but still, take care of ourselves.

As parents and caregivers, we always need to be sure we are in the right mental and emotional space to give our kids the daily support they need. I hope to encourage positive thinking and behaviors for families, inspire positive environments, as you learn to speak for yourself and become that True Advocate for your child.

Some families may be new to the spectrum and have many available resources within their reach, which I find to be awesome. I am concerned for those who are not able to find it as quickly or available in their community. Where do you start? How do you start? Whom can you see to ask questions? It's a lot to deal with from the very start.

But I believe in everyone. I believe that every child

of the spectrum and adult can overcome and

prosper, with the right tools, support and love.

"As a family, our journey on the 'autism express' has had many ups and downs. Autism is different for every individual; every family impacted by autism has a different ride"

-Holly Robinson-Peete

2

BREATHE

You got this

Take a deep breath. You did it! You took the initial
step of being an amazing parent. Please… take a
moment to absorb the energy. The moment you
decided to reach out for any guidance in your quest
for parenthood, you should commend yourself. As a
parent, it is not always easy to reach out for any
form of assistance, any help, so we often take on
full responsibility. Just the thought of processing
your child's diagnosis and feeling as though there

are little to no resources available to you is daunting, but I want to assure you that you are not alone. You are not alone on this journey.

For every autism diagnosis there are just as many caregivers, parents, grandparents, and loved ones who have the exact sentiments as you do:

How can I help my child on the spectrum? How can I be there to foster and encourage their growth to their highest potential? What resources will help my child and where may I find them?

Well, what exactly is Autism Spectrum Disorder

exactly? Autism, or Autism Spectrum Disorder,

refers to a broad range of conditions characterized

by challenges with social skills, repetitive behaviors

speech and non-verbal communication. What this

really means is, there is no one set of characteristics

that will fit the mold of each child. It will vary in

many fascinating ways.

If I must be honest, having the personal realization

that my two-year-old son was on the spectrum

really rushed my twenty-one-year-old, single parent

brain at a very intense level. I remember googling

his symptoms, profusely .

I was flooded with results. Different disorders,

opinions with self-written articles, YouTube videos,

and links to other websites had a chokehold on my

attention. I studied the documentaries

and books that were currently written at that time:

It wasn't until I took the online self-autism

screening, you know, the one where

you answer 'a b c or d' to a variety of emotional and

sensory-related questions. As I clicked to review the

results, recommending I have someone screen my

son for autism/Asperger or related disabilities, the

weight of feeling completely helpless rushed

over me. How can I do this? What can I do to help

my son? What resources will I have? Will my

family be understanding and supportive? And the

burning question: Where do I start? Having

these reoccurring questions live rent-free inside my brain drove me to a point of non-self-care, which is never good. When you become so absorbed that you disconnect from the world, your routine and any self-recognition, you put yourself in an environment that's nearly impossible to function in.

Little did I know, that the first step I needed to take when having that life-altering moment, the first step anyone should take when learning something new or receiving new life-changing information... Just Breathe. Yes, Breathe. Close your eyes - Inhale a solid deep breath - Exhale - Breathe. It seems so simple and rudimentary but it is indeed a tool you should keep on your belt.

We become so easily flustered, we are sometimes easily pressured by societal norms and we tend to over-analyze.

The first step in becoming the best parent you can be to your amazing gift is to 'Breathe'. Gain clarity. Meditate. Go for that quiet walk around the neighborhood. Having a clear and unclouded head will allow you to think much more reasonably. Your child is depending on you. Their little hearts may not understand today what is going on or why, but they are depending on you to show up with a smile. Finding doctors and therapists, looking for the right schools and resources, while also taking care of home life will become challenging…but you can do this! Just breathe.

Wake up every day and take that extra deep breath. Find the one thing to be thankful for. Set a reminder for a "breathing moment" during the day to reset yourself. Take a deep breath before bed and release all the day's stress, being sure to get a goodnights rest and wake up recharged. This simple but very powerful thing will certainly put you in the headspace to jumpstart this journey.

Breathe. You got this.

"Autism ISN'T the end of the world, it's the beginning of a whole new one"

-Autism Parent Magazine

3

Make a Plan

I know speaking for myself, I am the most sporadic and spontaneous person in my family. I grew up as an 'army brat', meaning, I moved frequently as my father was in the army. That also meant altering things constantly. With the help of my son, I have become the biggest planner in my family.

Mostly everything surrounding us once had a plan. Buildings, roadways, and trips to visit relatives, all normally require a basic plan.

Now, that is not to say everything goes as planned because ' happy accidents' have inspired some of the world's greatest discoveries (Edison +Apple=Gravity!).

However, we are "creatures of plans". Nine months of creation before birth, government constitutions and laws, a teacher giving her yearly lesson or even when we make that dreaded trip to the grocery store… we typically make a plan.

Plans provide a written, verbal, and visible goal for us to accomplish. Developing a plan or list of objectives to achieve will help give self-encouragement and self-empowerment on your Autism journey.

One step at a time, right?

Planning has changed and saved my life. I'm a 'first class f*ck up', in the flesh. I'm used to forgetting my hot tea on my car roof or that I scheduled a doctor's appointment on the same day as a dentists appointment. No-tor-i-ous. As my son has gotten older, he tends to remember our grocery list and what's needed in the home better than myself, and I absolutely love it! As you learn more about your child on the spectrum and their individualities, you will also see that they crave routine, order, and advance notice.

Being able to pre-plan before I make a trip to the grocery store saves time and is also a cool way to include your child in the shopping trip without it becoming an impossible task. I've always enjoyed having my son write out the list of weekly essentials with me, going over each item and its purpose to give him visuals. When we are at the store, his primary focus is more on finding the items on the list, rather than being distracted by all the shiny news items (wink).

Having a plan for that trip to the water park is better than arriving to find that there are no cabanas or bottled water available. Researching ahead, doing a little prep for outings or family get-together saves tears and jeers.

I've always found it useful to have an emergency backpack. That way, I know I have what I need in case things take longer, we run into any unexpected issues or…. plans simply change. I make sure to pack a bottle of water, a snack, and a change of clothes (you never know….and having dry clothes tops not having them at all), a small sandwich container-sized box of Lego minifigures or a puzzle for his hands and hand sanitizer.

Now I'm not saying go and write out your child's

retirement plans (yet…but we will get to that) and

over-exhaust yourself, no. I'm asking

you to 'breathe' first and start somewhere.

Anywhere. It's okay to start with small goals for

your child. Practicing using utensils. Writing with a

pencil. Eating a new vegetable. Signing how to say

the word "eat". Learning to ride a scooter. Positive

and achievable goals are great for esteem and

encouraging self- awareness.

Creating a plan for yourself, such as researching a

few doctors in the area who will better explain

resource options available to you or calling

your providers specialists and meeting with a

speech therapist. Start somewhere, and then work

towards it! One small accomplishment will

not only push you and your child further along on your autism journey but it gives you the self-appreciation that you 'are' doing what's best for them! It's easy to fall into a pit of despair, when you feel your immediate actions are not garnering 'immediate results'.

In time, crossing out every goal on your list, big or small, is a feat of its own."But what about those 'long term plans'?' Future goals for your child's education, therapy services, and medical care. Just reading about it or thinking about it can become exhausting, overwhelming, and quite frankly, I'm with you.

The mountains and rivers we must cross in order to provide a positive environment for our children to grow in seems unfeasible at times.

However; things are not always as they seem and it IS an obtainable goal. If you place your concerns and questions down on a piece of paper and list out every single obstacle you would like for them to overcome or a task to complete, with small steps and determination, it will indeed get done. It may not be today, tomorrow, next month, or next summer… but you have it on your list of goals and you are working towards it. It's not bouncing around in your head like a rubber headache, it's written and it's in motion for you to achieve.

Nine times out of ten…things will not go exactly as planned, in life. Ever. We make arrangements, appointments, and outlined detailed itineraries…

but Try as we might… SH*T HAPPENS!

That is OKAY! Embrace it.

No one is perfect and realistically, no one is expecting you to be.

It's okay to trip, make mistakes, double book or miss that appointment. It will happen more often than not, but I'm willing to bet you will learn from each mistake.

Breathe, and know you are not alone on this journey. We are all trying to figure it out, one day at a time.

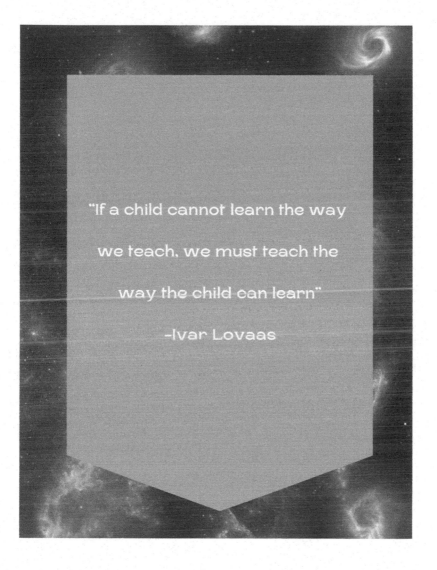

"If a child cannot learn the way

we teach, we must teach the

way the child can learn"

-Ivar Lovaas

4

Become an Advocate

Never be afraid to advocate for you child on the autism spectrum. Ever!

I know when I first hopped on the 'autism parenting train', I had no clue what advocate even meant.
The true definition of an advocate is a person who publicly supports or recommends a particular cause. Okay, simple enough… support autism and spread awareness. But I believe it's a little more than that. In a world that is ever-changing and developing, we still have neighbors, healthcare professionals, and institutions that are catching up to what autism truly means and how to care for our children, as well as, help the community.

This includes, but not limited to, doctors appts, school meetings, dentist appointments, airplane travel, childcare, or any public environment you may find you and your child in. Your voice, your instinct, your mindfulness, it DOES matter.

It's okay to not to go the prescription route and try a gluten free diet. It's okay to homeschool if you're uncomfortable with the learning environment for your children. It's okay to send your children to a private school. Do what you feel is best for your child.

One of the many responsibilities as parents is to secure a comfortable space and living environment for our children to grow and flourish. Whether it be at home, or away from home, we can always use our voice and become advocates for our children on the spectrum.

Everything we do should allow them to grow and establish their independency. Within that process, we should feel joy and comfort when advocating to others about the autism spectrum. It may not be a 'think piece' on the broad subject itself, but share what you know. Share what you have learned and experienced in your own personal parenting journey. You are relatable as a parent and as a person navigating this world, as is, your child on the spectrum, and your trials and triumphs.

Many of our encounters in life will be public or engaging others in our community. Simple interactions at doctors' appointments, grocery store visits and good ol' family get togethers, as well as social media, school and community settings. We will be engaging in front of and around other people. It is common that to have misperceptions or little to no understanding of what autism is or how to engage properly. Very often, as parents of a child on the spectrum, we must use our voices and courage to enlighten those around us. When we provide insight, personal stories, facts or just a light warning for our children and protecting their personal space- we are becoming advocates. It is important to note that an advocate does not necessarily mean someone who has an MBA degree in the subject.

It takes pure passion and support.

You possess the experience, you possess the knowledge. It's okay to share with your family that you prefer to come to the function a bit earlier and leave as the party becomes too much and may overstimulate your child. It's okay to separate yourself from judgmental eyes and comfort your child in the middle of Target because the intercom startled them.

I find it imperative that you use that same passion to express your concerns to your doctor and any provider. Having a list with you for clear communication on your concerns, calling beforehand to verify the check- in process and wait times are all things we are parental advocates of children on the spectrum can do. You can become a voice that makes a direct impact to your child's life…and even more special, that same voice can summon change to others without you even knowing it.

Advocacy expands beyond just public and social encounters, it is advocating for services in your community and even in your home. There are many resources available locally that promote advocacy and provide unity amongst the autism community.

5

Me Time

Easier said than done, right? Yeah, it is! But let me elaborate.

As parents, we dedicate a substantial amount of our time, love, energy and resources to our children. We are getting up early, going to bed when they are sleeping. Cooking, cleaning, and organizing appointments. Not to mention, navigating emotional breakdowns, rigorous health and wellness schedules, siblings and other family matters that go beyond just being a parent. It may seem as if, at every turn, your life has become "their life", in a sense. It's okay to give your best and 100% for your child.

What is not okay, is tearing yourself down in the

process of providing and being there for your child.

What is not okay, is losing yourself by filtering the

idea that everything is "more important"

than any form of self-care. Being a young single

parent of autism, I am very much guilty of throwing

myself, my heart, my time, and my energy

all into my child and not arranging any time for

myself, alone. You start to lose your self-identity

and become an outline of what you believe you

should be.

What's unhealthy about this the method is you

become unhappy and unfulfilled. You become

Guilty for wanting something more outside of

parenthood and closed off for not being able to share these raw emotions.

I experienced this personally as I started to see that avoiding self-care was affecting my daily life and my son. I didn't like that at all, so I changed it! I tried different things until I found something that gaveme personal happiness, made me feel energized and good about myself.

I got into cardio fitness, followed by 5K training for marathons and I love every minute of it. Not only do I have

an "excuse" to get away and clear my thoughts for the day, but it's something that makes me happy. Yes! I'm one of those. It gives me the feeling of accomplishment and breath of fresh air that I need. Even if it's not every day when I do choose to workout, it's a great personal experience that I'm able to collect my thoughts and harness good energy. That energy I bring back to my family and back to my son, ready and energized.

There are many healthy and fun outlets that do not have to break the bank or take you completely away from your day-to-day schedule. For those individuals with larger families or limited resources, you may find your happiness getting lost in a book or weekly magazine. Those stories could help draw you to new ideas and concepts. A garden, where you can get fresh air but remain close to home will give a sense of purpose and growth. Even finding arts and crafts or trying new recipes during a quiet nap time are great ideas to make you feel inspired and generate new ideas and momentum.

I highly encourage aiming to incorporate "me time "daily, whether it's early in the morning, during a car ride to work or at night when the house is 'quiet and still', at least once a day. Five minutes of meditation can make a days' worth of difference. We forget that although we have families, work, and home responsibilities, we still have a responsibility to ourselves to take care of our mind, body, and spirit.

6

Agree to Disagree

You know your child better than anyone else, of course. But!...

We do all know that overzealous parent or 'mom of 7' who has "been there, done that and worn the t-shirt". They would typically give out unsolicited parental advice at every opportunity. This may even include your own parents, family members and neighbors.

Although this may be coming from a good place of the heart, it's difficult to be receptive of someone's advice if they have not been in your shoes as a parent of someone on the autism spectrum.

As we know, no child is alike nor are our journeys as a parents. It's safe to say, we do come from a generation of elders who raised their families based on the "typical family structure". Mom, Dad, Child and a dog with picket fencing. Thankfully, we have made it to the future! Our families are different in every way, and it's beautiful to see and embrace. In this new day and age, different ideas and concepts to parenting are shared and at times utilized. This does not mean you must adhere to every article, social media post, and great-grand relatives idea of child rearing. You will go through an experience of your own 'trial and error' as a parent of autism.

Grammy award-winning artist Faith Evans is a proud parent and advocate of a beautiful boy on the autism spectrum. She has shared her own testimony to how challenging it was for her in the beginning to have any specialist diagnose her son. Many families are going through the same experience, where it seems we are having to plead and prove to others what we are seeing and engaging at home. It's a hard reality, but it is necessary.

Only we as parents and caregivers have the ability to speak up and advocate for our children. It may take some convincing and thorough 'picture painting', simply because the behaviors you describe are not displayed at the doctors' office during a visit in front of the doctor. It may seem exhausting and downright deeming because someone does not fully believe you about your own child.

It is okay to stand firm in the face of denial, agree to disagree and move forward. I love the idea of keeping a journal that highlights the patterns and habits of your daily experience as a parent and of your child. This journal will allow you to keep track of what exactly you are experiencing in the moment but also be able to clearly relay it to your medical professionals. I also love that it shows a detailed timeline of growth. Looking back on a journal like this will insightfully show a true measure of how far you have come as a family.

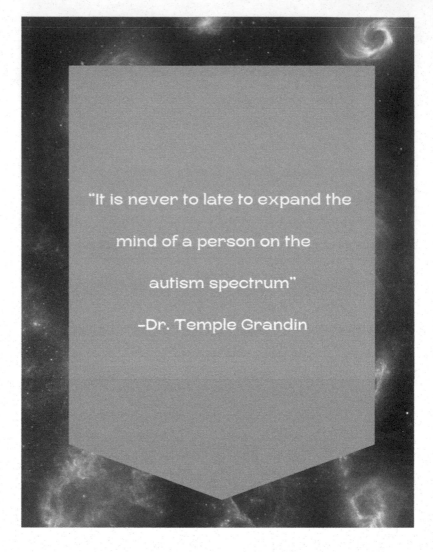

"It is never to late to expand the

mind of a person on the

autism spectrum"

-Dr. Temple Grandin

7

Early Intervention

I understand that not many families are able to receive access to resources near their community. It's unfortunate that we do not all have the same resources available to everyone within each country and community. My experience, as a single parent, I relied heavily on the sources that were available for free and within my reach. That is computer research, lower budget pediatricians and free diagnostic tests, reading books or watching documentaries. When it came to my son receiving early intervention care, I had to make the decision to move our family to a fast-paced city with more progression in the autism community.

It was not easy. I was a young mom in my early twenties, new area so that meant finding a new job as well as, diving headfirst into what was available for my son. It was the most difficult and the most rewarding decision I have made in my life.

Research shows that early diagnosis of and interventions for autism are more likely to have major long-term positive effects on symptoms and later skills. Early interventions occur at or before preschool age, as early as 2 or 3 years of age. In this period, a young child's brain is still forming,7 meaning it is more "plastic" or changeable than at older ages.

With early intervention, some children with autism make so much progress that they are no longer on the autism spectrum when they are older.

I remember back around 2012, my mother loved watching talk shows. I was in my very early 20s and had no interest in stopping to watch anything as we know life in your 20s moves fast. One evening as I was stopping by to visit her with my son, she asked me to stop and watch. I noticed right away who was on the screen, the beautiful and talented Mrs. Holly Robinson Peete. I recognized her from one of my favorite tv shows growing up, as she was the smart, attractive, and stylish single cast member, someone I admired! But this was not regarding her amazing acting, this was to highlight her own personal story and journey navigating as a mom of a beautiful and bright son on the autism spectrum.

I listened to what she had expressed, bringing more awareness to the community, and advocating for services, but what she expressed about early intervention was new to me. She explained, in a sense, that applied therapy services incorporated with early autism diagnosis can render very positive changes.

I found this to be quite interesting because up until that moment, I haven't heard of any way to help with autism. I remember reading a small passage or half page in our child development class about children with disabilities including autism and defining what autism is, but there was no mention of therapeutic services or positive hope. I remember feeling happy for them in that moment, thinking to myself "I'm so glad they were able to find help for their child", not knowing myself, that in that moment, I was approaching the starting line for the exact same marathon.

I credit a lot of my sons' progress to early intervention. Although he was nonverbal, he still had such an absorbent mind that just needed the right tools and instruction. We started with Pre-K, allowing someone to come into our home three times a week. She was a friendly face and talented therapist, someone my son enjoyed seeing. I'm so thankful for the days where my mother could be home with him more as I worked my first job in the medical field as a pharmacy technician.

I remember the transition from non-verbal, to some sounds and harmonization, to speaking words was very night and day. The day he called me by name (Jas. Not mom/mama, the "M's" were troublesome for him) and asked for something to "eat". I teared up immediately, because I knew and felt for the first time that if my son was ever in trouble or needed me, he could speak up for himself. That moment lives rent free in my mind and gave me so much more determination for Mars.

Nevertheless, intervention and applied therapy services at any age can be life altering for a child, teenager, or young adult. An official diagnosis can help unanswered questions get resolved and help family, friends or your employer to understand the difficulties you experience, and how they can make things a little easier. Some adults with ASD are happy self-diagnosing and adapting to life on their own terms, which is perfectly fine. It's up to each person to decide whether a late diagnosis could be beneficial for themselves.

"Autism doesn't come with an

instruction guide.

it comes with a

family who will never give up"

–Kerry Magro

8

Support System

Someone once said, "having a support system is like having a safety net below you at all times", and I agree with this. More often than not, we as parents place the responsibility solely on ourselves and negate help. This intensifies as a parent of a child on the spectrum. We take on the responsibility of parent, teacher, caregiver, cook, live-in therapist, referee (if more than one kid is in the home), personal shopper, event/ outing planner, nurse, friend and so much more. Sometimes we may feel as if we are obligated to juggling all these tasks on our own.

I am here to say, that it's okay to have a support system. It's okay to ask for help from family, close friends or hiring a trusted nanny. Although, there may come extra responsibility while caring for a child on the spectrum, those caring methods can be taught and learned. Grandparents are almost always thrilled to be involved with the growth and development of their grandchild, and they do not feel burdened (thankfully!)

I think back to the times my mother and stepfather (affectionately known to Mars as his 'Gigi and pop pop) hosted soul sliding line dance classes in Tampa, Florida and they would have my son with them every Wednesday and Sunday, due to me being in school or at work at the time. I think back to the exposure he had to seeing new faces and being able to express himself comfortably in a slightly changing but consistent weekly setting. I know without a doubt, those delicate moments set the base foundation for allowing my son to feel comfortable speaking to others and engaging. I know that being an only child has exposed him to various environments that has helped develop his language beyond my wildest imaginations and I'm thankful for every bit of it. I knew therapy and education were top priority but support from my family was the icing on the cake.

Whether family, friends, coworker, or long-time 'trusted neighbor'... having someone wholeheartedly available for venting or an emergency is essential to your own growth and development. We may feel as though this is our responsibility to handle on our own but it's normal to have a team behind you when approaching parenthood with autism and in general. You know that saying "it takes a village".

I have two brothers and one sister that I grew up with all over the United States, we moved as army brats. We practically raised each other, so we know each other well…but autism was new, and I introduced it as "we raise him no differently and give him the same love we have for each other". Granted, they did not breakout the pamphlets and psychology books, not exactly. They were able to attend a couple of Autism awareness walks with us in Florida and had hands on experience with babysitting him during the summer. It's not perfect, but it's real love and real support. That, I am thankful for.

"As a dad on the Autism

Spectrum. you have to put
away

your ego"

-Sylvester Stallone

Peter T.

Son, Alex, Autism Spectrum Disorder

Bowie, Maryland

On raising two sons, one on the spectrum and one that is not: For me, it was learning that the challenges he faced when trying to communicate was greater than my understanding. He started speaking when hit age four or five, and I was so happy. Honestly, I was so busy life, divorce in motion, and I never fully realized "Alex does not talk that much". His older brother, Ryan, was very talkative and always talked for Alex. Ryan would say "Oh hey! I'm Ryan, this is my brother Alex" and Alex would just nod his head in agreeance and smile. So that's how it started for me, recognizing his challenges, and acting on them.

We had to start to tell his older brother Ryan "Hey, you have to let Alex speak for himself". Although, however, Ryan does it to this day when he looks out for his brother and habitually may speak for him, Alex has a beautiful mind of his own. It's amazing to watch him grow and see myself in my son. Alex drinks ensure constantly, so I know he will be 'built' like his father, and I tell his older brother "Watch out! You may be the little brother' one day!

From a man's standpoint, it does start out as just fear because you don't know, and you fear the 'unknown'. Then you kind of must put your mind in the game and realize that we can all be taught and figure this out together. So, when you start to see the glimpses of triumphs and "small wins" it is amazing to me. I'm very happy that I get to see his growth, not only through things that bond us such as video games and movies but watching him learn to read.

I remember digging up his older brother's Dr. Suess books and before, Alex would just look at the pictures and ask "Dad, what is that?". He would say the words that he knew and ask about the words he was not familiar with, sounding out the letters. For Alex, I know that perceptually he is going to thrive because of the progress he makes on his own every day. It's always the simplest things that mean the most.

"Autism is proof that

love does not

need words"

-Anonymous

Jason

Son, Bug, Autism Spectrum Disorder

Lakeland, Florida

On raising a son on the autism spectrum:

There was a point and time in my life when I was

consumed with so much negativity and darkness.

Angry at myself, angry at my choices, and angry at

life, until my son entered my life. I remember,

vividly, he came over to me one day as a very

young child, climb up onto my chest, and laid his

head on my chest while placing his ear directly on

my heartbeat. He would fall asleep peacefully that

way. This is when I started to write in my little

journal, which helps me process the emotions

and thoughts that I have every day. Bug became my little 'guiding light bug", through the darkness. Everything I had experienced up until that moment seemed so small once I realized the totality of how much greater my life is just by having him in it. Just by being his dad. As he got older, he didn't like the term "Light Bug" so naturally, we dropped the 'light' and 'Bug' became his nickname. He guided his daddy out of a darkness I couldn't see my own self out of. I knew that I had to be the man that I would like for him to become, no less.

Q: What would you say is something that you and Bug bond over?

A: Cooking, for sure. We grill together and watch movies

If I'm not at work, I am with Bug. We literally do everything together and I make sure we have a "father-son day" at least once a week. It's where we go out, and this is how I somewhat got him adjusted to being in big crowds and whatnot because he couldn't do it before. So, what I do is, I would take Bug out to lunch (and I let him pick the place). Afterward, we may head to a place like a courtyard at the mall. Not totally "inside", but we are surrounded by people and in a common area and we sit, and we just talk. Although there are a lot of people there, he is focused on me and at the same time, he is getting used to being around hundreds of people. In the beginning, we could not stay there long at all: maybe three or four minutes. Now, we can get up to two hours! The progress, just by something small and consistent, moves me. So, I make sure we have that time every week and it's just "daddy and me" and we do whatever makes him happy. Fitting in the time can be challenging as a single dad because I do work extremely hard to support Bug and give him everything that he needs, but it would be an understatement to say that it's not worth it. I would not change anything because Bug is the best part of me, and I would not even be who I am today without him.

Afterword

If I would like to sum up the key take away from what I've shared in this book, it's to embrace each and every moment of you and your child's autism journey. The challenges will come, as with many other things in life, but do not neglect enjoyment of your own unique experience.

ACKNOWLEDGEMENTS

Editors - A special thank you to Mark Antony Rossi. I appreciate your genuine energy.

Supporters - Thank you 'Team Jamari' for your yearly support and advocation for autism. Having the love and support of this family has inspired me to serve the autism community in many ways. Thank you!